Wonders

Program Authors

Diane August

Donald R. Bear

Janice A. Dole

Jana Echevarria

Douglas Fisher

David Francis

Vicki Gibson

Jan Hasbrouck

Margaret Kilgo

Jay McTighe

Scott G. Paris

Timothy Shanahan

Josefina V. Tinajero

Mc
Graw
Hill
Education

M000291495

Cover and Title pages: Nathan Love

www.mheonline.com/readingwonders

Send all inquiries to:
McGraw-Hill Education
2 Penn Plaza
New York, NY 10121

ISBN: 978-0-07-677574-3
MHID: 0-07-677574-7

Printed in the United States of America.

4 5 6 7 8 9 RMN 20 19 18 17 16

B

Unit 4 Around the Neighborhood

The Big Idea: What do you know about the people and places in your neighborhood?

Week 1 · Time for Work 4

Phonics: *Oo* 6
Words to Know: *you* 7
Tom on Top! Nonfiction 8
Writing and Grammar: Informative Text 16

Week 2 · Meet Your Neighbors . . . 18

Phonics: *Dd* 20
Words to Know: *do* 21
Sid Fiction 22
Writing and Grammar: Informative Text 30

Week 3 · Pitch In 32

Phonics: Review *i, n, c, o, d* 34
Words to Know: Review *to, and, go, you, do* 35
I Can, You Can! Fiction 36
Writing and Grammar: Informative Text 44

SOCIAL STUDIES

(t) ML Harris/Iconica/Getty Images; (c) Nancy Cote; (b) Kathi Ember

Essential Question

What do people use to do their jobs?

Go Digital!

Tanya Constantine/Blend Images/Getty Images

4

On the Job!

COLLABORATE

Talk About It

What tools does
this worker use?

Say the name of each picture.

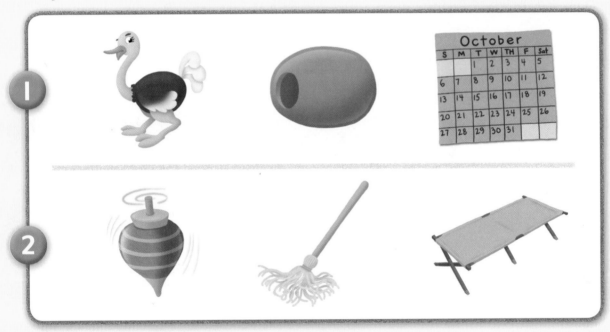

Read each word.

3   **on**   **tot**   **top**

4   **pot**   **Mom**   **not**

Read Together

you

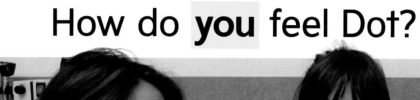

How do **you** feel Dot?

Do **you** like milk?

7

Tom On Top!

Can **you** see a ?
firehouse

(t)Stockbyte/Getty Images; (b)Jenna Riggs

I can see a 🚒.
fire truck

I can see a  .

I can see a  .
hose

I can see a  hat.

I can see a pot.

I can see Tom on top!

Write About the Text

Tom On Top!

Pages 8–15

Michael

I responded to the prompt: **Write about a nurse's office. Use "Tom On Top!" as a model.**

Student Model: *Informative Text*

Details
I used details in my story as in "Tom on Top!"

A Nurse on the First Floor

Can you see a nurse's office?

I can see a clean room.

Grammar
The word **clean** is an **adjective.** It describes the room.

16

I can see a chart. ◄

I can see a bandage. ◄

I can see a nurse!

Topic
My sentences tell about the things in a nurse's office.

Your Turn

COLLABORATE

Write a selection called "A Teacher in Class IA" using "Tom on Top!" as a model.

Go Digital!
Write your response online.
Use your editing checklist.

17

Essential Question

Who are your neighbors?

Go Digital!

Hello, Neighbor!

Talk About It

What do good neighbors do?

19

Dd

Say the name of each picture.

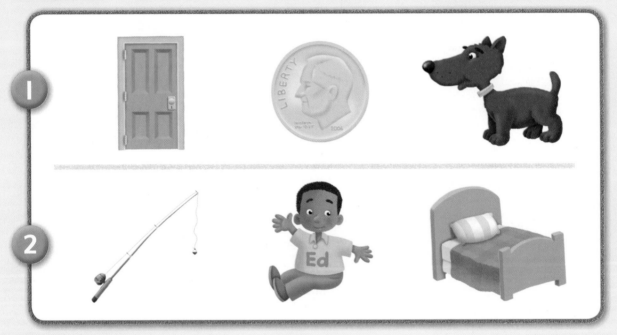

1

2

Read each word.

3 **dot**   **mad**   **dip**

4 **cod**   **dad**   **Dan**

Read Together

do

We **do** want to go!

I can help you **do** it.

(t)IT Stock/PunchStock; (b)Daniel Pangbourne/Digital Vision/Getty images

21

Sid

Nancy Cote

Do Sid and Mom like it?

Nancy Cote

23

Sid and Mom do like it!

Nancy Cote

Dan can tap, tap on a .

door

Dot can tap, tap on a .

door

Dot and Dan can sip.

Nancy Cote

Tod can tap, tap on a .

door

28

Sid and Tod pat a .

ball

29

Nancy Cote

Write About the Text

Pages 22–29

Emma

I answered the prompt: **What can you tell about the new neighbors?**

Student Model: *Informative Text*

Describing Words
I used the word **friendly** to tell about the neighbors.

The new neighbors are friendly. The neighbors are happy to say hello.

Tetra Images-Mike Kemp/Getty Images

Details
I used story information to tell about the neighbors.

The neighbors bring nice things.
Tod brings a big, orange ball.
Tod likes to play ball.

Grammar
The words **big** and **orange** are adjectives.

Your Turn

What are good neighbors like?

Go Digital!
Write your response online.
Use your editing checklist.

31

Essential Question

How can people help to make your community better?

Go Digital!

Talk About It

COLLABORATE

How are these children helping their community?

Let's Help Out!

Review Letter Sounds

Say the name of each picture.

Read each word.

3 **dot**　　　**did**　　　**cot**

4 **nip**　　　**Don**　　　**nod**

Review Words

Read the words and sentences.

1. **to**   **and**   **go**

2. **you**   **do**

3. **Do you** want **to go** to the garden?

4. We can dig **and** water the plants.

Taxi/Getty Images

35

I Can, You Can!

Mom **and** I **go** **to** a .
beach

Kathi Ember

I can pat, pat, pat on top.

Can **you** pat it?

Kathi Ember

I can tip, tip it on top.

Don can see it.

Kathi Ember

I can pat, pat, pat on top.

We can **do** it!

Write About the Text

Pages 36–43

Ben

I answered the question: **Look at the illustrations in "I Can, You Can!" What can you tell about Don?**

Student Model: *Informative Text*

Don likes to help.

Don is friendly.

Don works hard.

Grammar

The word **friendly** is an **adjective.** It tells about Don.

Clues

I used the pictures to figure out what Don is like.

44

Don is happy.
He is proud of the castle.

**Specific
Words**
I used the
word **proud**
to show how
Don feels.

Your Turn

Look at the
illustrations in "I Can,
You Can!" What can
you tell about the
little girl?

Go Digital!
Write your response online.
Use your editing checklist.

45